Mary's House

BY THE SAME AUTHOR

The Donald Carroll Interviews

The Insider's Guide to Turkey

New Poets of Ireland

Why Didn't I Say That?

The Best Excuse

Co-authored with Edward Lucie-Smith

Movements in Modern Art

Co-authored with Quentin Crisp

Doing It with Style

Donald Carroll

Mary's House

The extraordinary story behind
the discovery of the house where the
Virgin Mary lived and died

VERITAS BOOKS
LONDON

To
Louise

First published in Great Britain in 2000 by Veritas Books
17 Avenue Mansions, London NW3 7AX
www.veritasbooks.co.uk

A CIP catalogue record for this book is available from the British Library.

Special acknowledgments to Gülsen Kahraman and Ayçe Dörtok.

Set in 11/15pt Baskerville
Designed by Rob Norridge/Norridge Walker Design Associates
Production by Anderson Fraser Partnership
Printed and bound in The Netherlands by Chevalier International

ISBN: 0-9538188-0-2

Contents

The House on Nightingale Mountain

Now there was standing by the cross of Jesus His mother and His mother's sister, Mary of Cleophas, and Mary Magdalene.
When Jesus, therefore, saw His mother and the disciple standing by, whom He loved, He said to His mother, 'Woman, behold thy son.' Then He said to the disciple, 'Behold thy mother.'
And from that hour the disciple took her unto his home.

St John 19:25-27

This is the last mention of Mary in the Bible. After this, as a mortal, as a woman, she disappears into history.

Fortunately, however, she didn't disappear without trace. It is known, for example, that in the years following the stoning to death of St Stephen in 37 AD, when the persecution of Christians in Jerusalem became particularly severe, St John took Mary with him to Ephesus, on the Aegean coast of present-day Turkey. Already one of the greatest cities of the Roman Empire, Ephesus was the capital of the Roman province of Asia, and was soon to become, in the words of the nineteenth-century French historian Ernest Renan, "the Second Province of God". It was from here that the Apostles effectively

Detail of The Madonna with the Pomegranate by Botticelli

launched Christianity; it was here that St Paul preached for three years and wrote his letters to the Corinthians; it was here that St John wrote his Gospel. And it was here, following St John's death, that first a memorial and later a great basilica were built over his grave.

But whatever became of Mary? Understandably, St John and the others responsible for her well-being were not keen to draw attention to her presence in Ephesus, a city dominated by the mighty Temple of Artemis, dedicated to the worship of the Mother Goddess. Besides, it was *their* job, not hers, to challenge the paganism of the Romans and spread the news of Christianity. Her role was simply to keep a low profile, for her own sake. Alas for historians down the centuries, she succeeded all too well.

Nonetheless, she didn't vanish from the thoughts of the growing Christian community in Ephesus, who kept alive the memory of Mary's time among them. Thus it came as no surprise when, in the fourth century, the first church in Christendom to be dedicated to the Virgin Mary was in Ephesus. (It is worth noting that at that time a church could only be dedicated to a saint if that person had actually lived there or been martyred there.) Nor was it a coincidence that when the Third Ecumenical Council convened in 431 AD to proclaim Mary to be the Mother of God, the Council was held in the Church of the Virgin Mary in Ephesus.

Still, it was not until the late nineteenth century that anybody made the effort to find out exactly how and where Mary had lived – in other words, to connect the divine Mary, the Queen of Heaven, to the earthly Mary, the sorrowing old lady who spent her last days away from the tumult that accompanied the birth of the religion that would ultimately exalt her above all women.

The man who made the first effort to locate Mary's final home on earth was a Parisian priest, Abbé Julien Gouyet. Father Gouyet had come upon a book which recounted verbatim the visions of a bedridden German nun and stigmatic who had died half a century earlier. In these visions the nun described in considerable detail the house where Mary died as well as its location. Father Gouyet was enthralled by the book, and in 1881 went to Ephesus to see if he could find the house for

himself, following the nun's directions. He found it near the summit of Bülbül Dağı, "Nightingale Mountain", just south of Ephesus. Or at least he thought he had found it, but when he reported his discovery to his superiors in Paris and in Rome a veil of silence was quickly drawn over the matter. Nobody took his claims seriously. It was another ten years before a series of expeditions to the house, in 1891, collected enough evidence to convince the Vatican that the house was not just any old ruin, and a further several years of excavations and study before scholars were prepared to accept the likelihood that the house on Nightingale Mountain was indeed Mary's house.

At this point I should confess that my initial reaction to the "holy version" of the house's origins was not dissimilar to that of the Church. Even after several visits I remained cheerfully skeptical. After all, it

Pietà by Bartolome Bermejo

seemed hardly credible that an ancient stone building, however remote, however small and unprepossessing, could go unnoticed for 1800 years. And one's credulity was stretched even further upon learning that the house was first "sighted" by a sickly nun in Germany who had had visions which led to the house's discovery. Finally, if the discovery was the epochal event it was supposed to be, why was there not a single book about the house available either at the site or in bookshops in nearby towns?

On the other hand, one had to concede that even fabled Troy had managed to disappear for 3,000 years, while the splendid marble city of Ephesus itself had vanished from sight for five centuries. Moreover, the discovery of Troy in 1873 by Heinrich Schliemann was only made possible by Schliemann's stubborn determination to follow the clues in

The rebuilt house as it stands today

the *Iliad*, not the most reliable work of historiography, while Ephesus would have remained buried underground if an English engineer and amateur archaeologist, John Turtle Wood, had not followed the description of a procession he found on a fragment of stone. So perhaps one should not be tempted to judge the authenticity of a discovery by the manner in which it was discovered.

That still left the question of why there was apparently no book on the subject. There were the usual tourist brochures and booklets, which either repeated or contradicted each other, in wonderfully eccentric English, but there was no one reliable account of what actually took place on this mountainside a century ago – or, for that matter, twenty centuries ago. With my curiosity now fueled by frustration, I turned to the Internet, and to booksearch agencies, and to the best antiquarian booksellers. At first the results were discouraging, but gradually pieces of information began to surface, some in English but most in French or German or Turkish, rather like shards of glass in different shapes and colors that you hope, and then start to believe, will form a stained-glass window if reconstructed properly.

So do I now believe my own reconstruction? Yes, to this extent: I know the facts of the story have been assembled with a scrupulous regard for accuracy, and I know that in no instance has history been reworked to accommodate the demands of faith. Nonetheless, it has to be admitted that the evidence for Mary's residency on Nightingale Mountain, however detailed and impressive, remains circumstantial, and it will probably always remain so. In that way it is no different from any other unprovable proposition at the heart of religion: it requires a leap of faith. That's what faith is for.

But in the case of Mary's house, it is the shortest leap I know.

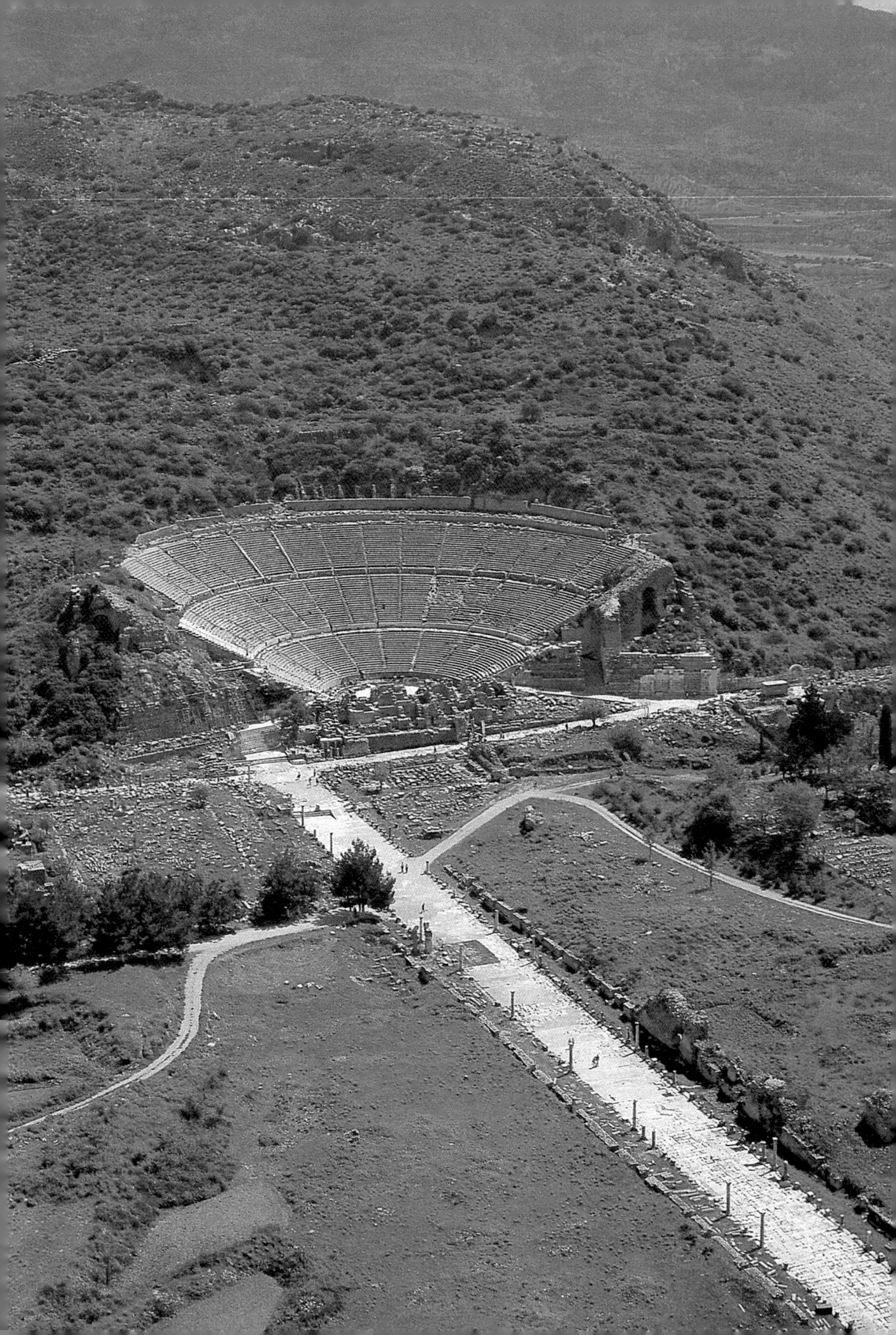

Chapter one

The Ephesus of Mary and St John

In the years immediately following the Crucifixion, the little sect of troublemakers known as Christians enjoyed a period of relative tolerance in Jerusalem. But as their numbers and influence expanded, the patience of the Jewish authorities shrank until, in 37 AD, it disappeared altogether. That year saw the martyrdom of St Stephen, and with it the beginning of active persecution of Jerusalem's Christian community. Over the next five years the persecution became more intense, reaching its climax when Herod Agrippa I ascended the throne in 42 AD and ordered the imprisonment of St Peter and the beheading of St James, the brother of St John.

By then, however, most of the Christians, including St John and the Virgin Mary, had fled. The majority escaped into Judea and Samaria, but those who like St John were charged with spreading the message of Jesus went much further afield. In St John's case, he went to Ephesus and, true to his commitment to the dying Jesus, took Mary with him – as well as Mary Magdalene, and several others of the faithful.

One can scarcely imagine the hardships that must have accompanied a journey of that length, in those conditions, over that terrain. Mary especially must have suffered during their long flight out of the Holy Land; she would have been in her sixties by this time. Nor can one imagine the reaction of this little group of refugees when they first

Harbor Street leading to the Grand Theatre

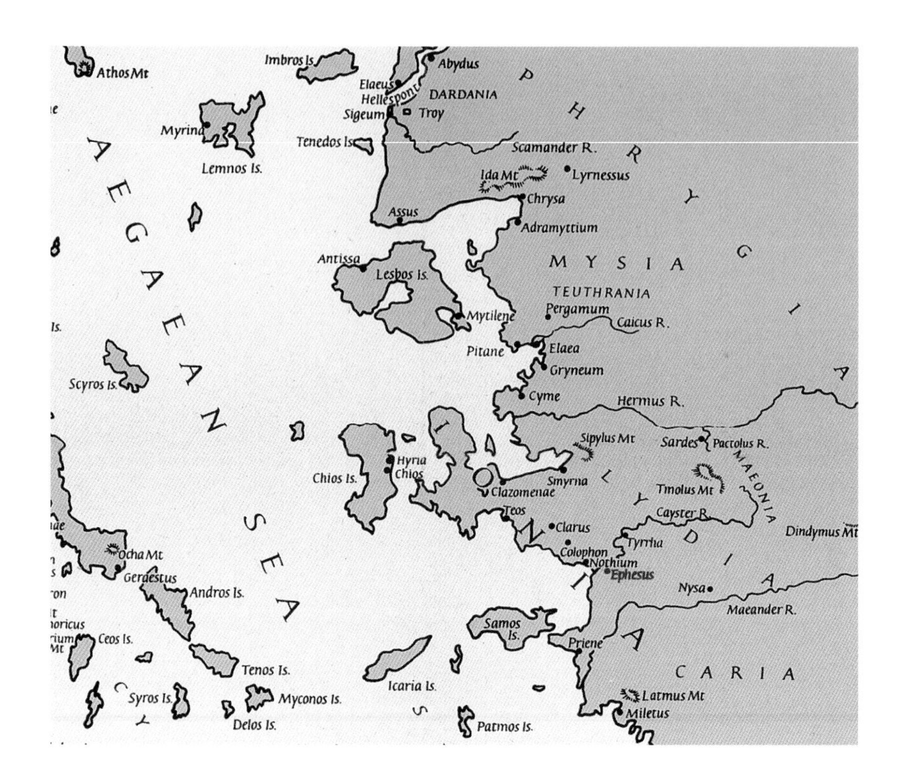

beheld the splendor of Ephesus. Here was the greatest city of the East, the financial center of the Roman Empire, home of the world's first bank, a city of vast wealth and a quarter of a million citizens. The effect must have been overwhelming.

Approaching Ephesus along what is now called the Virgin Mary Road, they would have been confronted with the massive city walls which had been built by Alexander the Great's general and successor, Lysimachus, in the third century BC. To their left the walls would have run along the upper slopes of Nightingale Mountain. Entering through the Magnesia Gate, they would have come first upon the State Agora, a huge public square surrounded by buildings that served as the city's administrative center. Along its northern side, facing the road, was a giant basilica which housed the law courts. The square itself, a semi-sacred area where political and religious meetings were held, would

Right, the lay-out of Ephesus today

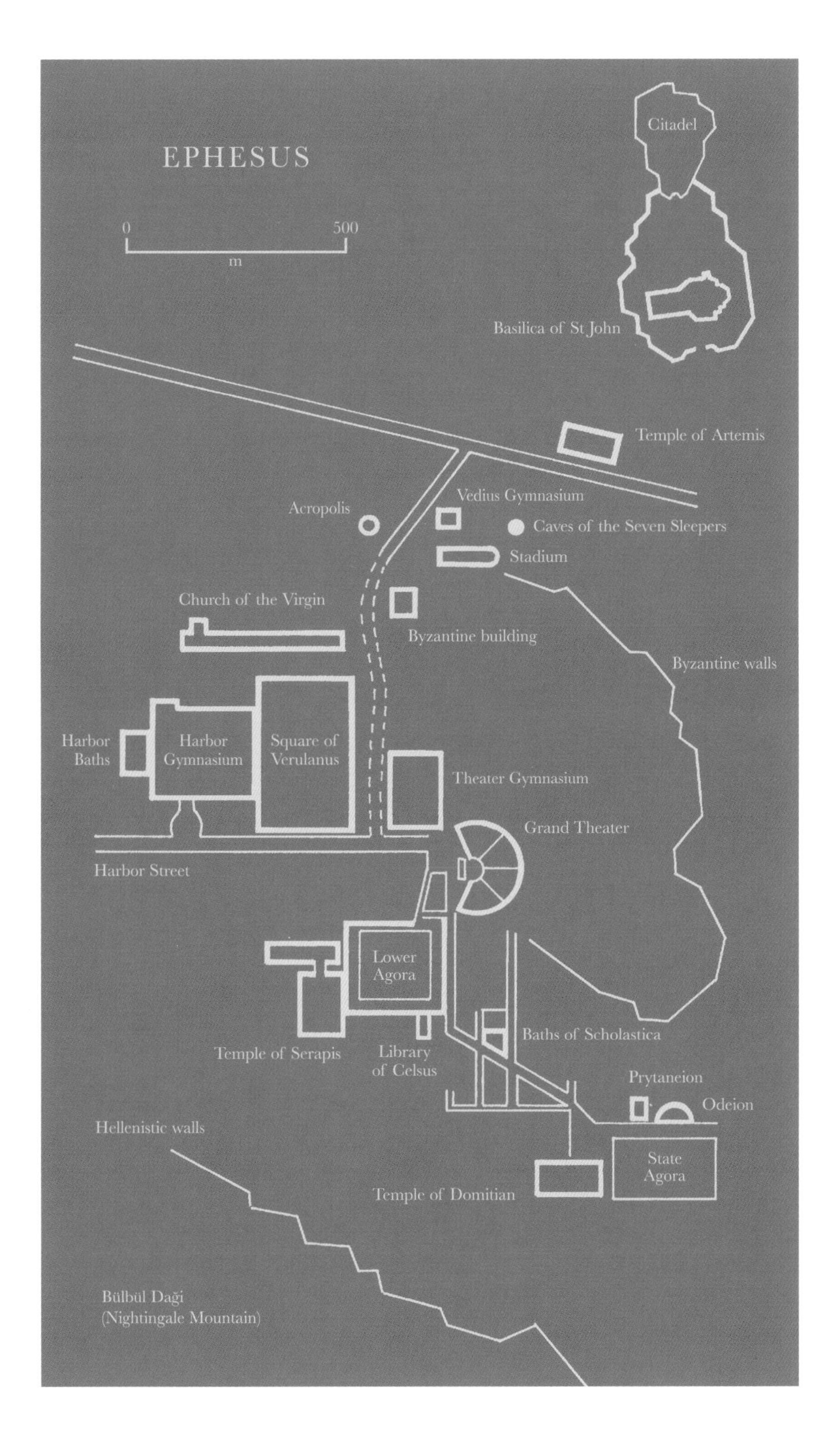
EPHESUS
0
500
m
Citadel
Basilica of St John
Temple of Artemis
Vedius Gymnasium
Acropolis
Caves of the Seven Sleepers
Stadium
Church of the Virgin
Byzantine building
Byzantine walls
Harbor Baths
Harbor Gymnasium
Square of Verulanus
Theater Gymnasium
Grand Theater
Harbor Street
Lower Agora
Baths of Scholastica
Temple of Serapis
Library of Celsus
Prytaneion
Odeion
Hellenistic walls
State Agora
Temple of Domitian
Bülbül Daği
(Nightingale Mountain)

have been hidden from view, but the serious hubbub coming from it would have signaled its importance. Just past the State Agora, on the other side of the street, were the eight large Doric columns of the Prytaneion, behind which the eternal flame of Ephesus burned day and night. Further on were the impressive monuments and fountains that together formed Rome's imperial signature.

They would then have come to the archway that opened on to the Street of the Curetes, named after a special order of priests devoted to Artemis. This led down into the center of the city. Lining the street were marble statues of Ephesian dignitaries, and it was flanked on both sides by porticoes paved with mosaics. Opening on to these porticoes were buildings on each side, mostly public or commercial on the right, private and residential on the left. Among the buildings on the right were the city brothel, the public latrine, in which the toilets were cut into marble benches arranged along each of the walls, and the public baths. On the left, extending up the hillside, were the villas of the rich and powerful.

Turning right at the bottom of the Street of the Curetes, Mary and her companions would have been faced with one of the most staggering vistas in the ancient world. On the left was the monumental,

Above, the triple-arched Mazeus and Mithridates Gate
Left, mosaic paving in the Street of the Curetes

triple-arched Mazeus and Mithridates Gate through which one entered into the Commercial Agora, the city's marketplace. Along its exterior, stretching over a hundred meters in front of them, were rows of shops behind porticoed galleries. Just beyond the Agora, across the street to the right, was the Grand Theatre, a massive amphitheatre built into the hillside with seating for 24,000 spectators. And ahead in the distance was the awesome Temple of Artemis, one of the Seven Wonders of the World, 155 meters long and 55 meters wide, with a double row of monolithic columns 22 meters high surrounding its walls, the largest building in the world ever to have been constructed entirely of marble.

Then, sweeping from the Grand Theatre down to the harbor, there was the Harbor Street (later renamed the Arcadian Way after the early fifth-century Emperor Arcadius), a wide colonnaded avenue paved in marble and lined with shops behind enormous columns. Between the shops and the columns were porticoed pedestrian walkways covered in elaborate mosaics. The street, which was over 500 meters long, was lit at night by 50 large torches – making Ephesus, along with Rome and Antioch, one of only three cities of antiquity to have street lighting. But the Harbor Street was more than just a lavish mercantile thoroughfare; because it ended at the busy harbor, which was always filled with ships from all over the known world, it was also the ceremonial entranceway to the city through which emperors and potentates and other historical figures, including Antony and Cleopatra, had passed when they visited Ephesus.

It was in a house north of the Harbor Street, near a large sports arena, that Mary is thought to have stayed during her first months in Ephesus while St John was having a house built for her on Nightingale Mountain. Obviously, it would be pointless to speculate here on the exact circumstances of Mary's life in Ephesus, but two things can be said with a degree of certainty. Firstly, and most importantly, she is unlikely to have felt herself at risk from the local authorities. The city's government was notable for its religious tolerance, allowing Jews, for example, despite their alien monotheism, to establish synagogues and practice their religion openly without interference. Also, of course, evangelical Christianity (in the form of St Paul) had yet to reach Ephesus, and thus hardly represented anything worth worrying about.

So there was no fear of persecution, as there had been in Jerusalem. Secondly, Mary's physical comfort is likely to have been much greater in Ephesus than it had been before. This, after all, was one of the few cities in the world where most of the houses had running water, and where every conceivable kind of food, clothing and household item was readily available.

Most necessities could be found in the Commercial Agora. Bread, vegetables, grain, meat, fish, live animals, olive oil, wine, honey, salt and Arabian herbs and spices could all be purchased there, in addition to a whole range of household goods including copper kitchenware, bronze tables, marble objects, ceramics, glassware, stools, pitchers, bowls, amphoras and oil lamps. For those with more money to spend, there were silks, perfumes and jewelry made of precious stones. One could even buy labor there, because slaves and freemen who wanted a job would go there at sunrise and wait to be selected by someone who needed a worker for the day.

A seventeenth-century impression of the Temple of Artemis

For all the city's tradesmen and street vendors and shopkeepers, they were still greatly outnumbered by farm workers. Agriculture was very important to the Ephesian economy, and many of the rich city-dwellers made their fortunes from farming the land around Ephesus. That, however, did not put them among the most highly-regarded (or highly-paid) citizens. These positions were reserved for those who added significantly to the beauty of the city. At the top were the sculptors, followed by architects, makers of ceramics (especially vase painters), weavers and dyers, stone cutters, silversmiths, jewelers, ivory cutters, blacksmiths and glaziers. Doctors were important, of course, but not much more so than barbers. And it is wistfully pleasing to note that lawyers were expected to provide their services free, although they were allowed to charge a symbolic fee.

Regardless of their social or economic status, the one luxury available to all Ephesians was that afforded by the public baths. There

An eighteenth-century interpretation of the interior of the Temple of Artemis

were separate baths for men and women, though women were allowed to bathe in the men's baths if they went early in the morning. Three stories high, the baths included an apoditarium where visitors disrobed, a sudotorium for sweating, a caldarium (hot room) for massages and bathing, a tepidarium for resting, and a frigidarium, with a cold pool for a refreshing splash before leaving. The baths were heated by an ingenious system known as hypocausis. There was a furnace near the caldarium where the water was boiled in huge cauldrons; the steam and hot air was then carried away through lead or ceramic pipes placed in the walls and under the floors of the rooms to be heated.

For the rich, a visit to the baths could take up the entire afternoon. After a spell in the sudotorium, they would move on to the caldarium to bathe and to be scrubbed and massaged and finally covered in scent by their servants. Then they would retire to the tepidarium to sit with their friends and discuss all the issues and solve all the problems of the day. This covered a lot of ground in the years after Mary arrived in the city: the assassination of Caligula by his Praetorian Guard in 42 AD, the Roman invasion of Britain and the establishment of a settlement called Londinium on the banks of the Thames in 43, the controversial preaching in Ephesus by St Paul from 53 onwards, the poisoning of Claudius by his wife Agrippina in 54, followed by her own murder in 59 at the behest of her son Nero, who then had his wife Octavia killed in 62, before killing himself in 68, two years before the revolt of the Jews in 70, a series of jolts that ran through the Empire and climaxed with the disappearance of Pompeii under the ash of Vesuvius in 79. A lot to talk about.

And when the rich weren't luxuriating in the baths, they were luxuriating in their sumptuous villas, many of which were just across the Street of the Curetes. Known as "The Houses on the Slopes", they had modest facades and were only accessible via the sidestreets or the streets behind them up the hill. Most were three stories, and inside they were palatial. Each was built around a large marble courtyard, which could be up to 50 meters square, uncovered to let in the daylight, usually with a fountain in the middle, and surrounded by marble columns. The top floor was always occupied by bedrooms with brightly colored frescoes, many of which were scenes from the comedies of Menander and the tragedies of Euripides. The ground floor was reserved for the "public rooms": the dining room, the living room, and the main hall where the hosts received their guests on floors covered with intricate, beautiful mosaics. On the bottom floor were the servants' quarters, the kitchen, the bath, and a room with enough toilets and wash basins to accommodate several people at once. All of these rooms, too, including the lavatory, were covered in frescoes. Every house had its own cistern or well, in addition to the municipal running water, and each was centrally heated, using the same hypocaust system that heated the public baths.

In addition to the amenities offered by the public baths, another pleasure enjoyed by rich and poor alike, though of course not in the same measure, was that of eating well. Their basic diet revolved around dishes made from wheat flour together with onion, garlic, and cheese. On top of this, both fish and meat, especially pork, were abundant and affordable by everyone. Poorer families, however, usually had just two meals a day. The morning meal typically consisted of bread soaked with wine, honey, olives, dates, salad, perhaps a little fruit, and whatever special dishes they chose to prepare. The evening meal usually featured a selection of hot and cold dishes accompanied by watered-down wine. All food in poorer households was eaten with the fingers.

Meals in the homes of wealthy Ephesians were naturally much grander affairs. Dinner guests would be expected to leave their sandals or shoes in the entrance hall, and their feet would be washed by a servant (usually a slave) before they entered the dining room. A typical meal would then consist of three courses. It would begin with a drink of wine mixed with honey, which was thought to aid digestion. This was followed by any number of appetizers: beetroot, cabbage, leeks, lettuce, mushrooms, meatball soup, oysters, salted fish, and occasionally snails. For the main course there would be either fresh fish or meat such as lamb, goat, beef, pork, wild boar, and duck. The dishes were almost always cooked in olive oil with salt and pepper, to which could be added

The courtyard of one of the "Houses on the Slopes"

one or more of their favorite herbs such as parsley, fennel and mint, or spices such as cumin and cinnamon. For dessert there would be a selection of sweets and fruits. All of this was washed down with heroic quantities of wine – which, like the humbler wine of the poor, was inevitably watered down.

Every meal, whether consumed by the rich or the poor, had three things in common: wine, honey, and salt. Indeed, Ephesus was famous for its wine – there was a Wine Festival every year on the 19th of August – and its honey. (The bee, which was the ancient symbol of Ephesus, even appeared on some of its coins.) As for salt, it was considered so important that even the poorest families would make sacrifices just to be able to buy a silver salt container for the table.

In the matter of dress, there was little to distinguish the wealthy from their less privileged fellow citizens. The basic everyday garment was the tunic, made of a mixture of cotton and wool in the case of ordinary people and of expensive silk in the case of the more affluent. Some tunics had sleeves, others were sleeveless; all were belted at the hip. Men's tunics were short and consisted of a single piece of cloth. Women's were long and consisted of two pieces of cloth, one worn on top of the other. And whereas the men dressed uniformly in white, the women wore a variety of colors, of which blue, violet, and saffron yellow were the most popular. The familiar Roman toga was seldom worn except during festivals, sacrifices, and public holidays. Manual workers and slaves tended to wear a brown, sack-shaped garment called a cucullus which extended from the neck to the knees.

By the time Mary got to Ephesus, the men no longer wore beards, but they had joined in one of the quirkier fashions of the time: the vogue for blond hair. Men as well as women were to be seen with dyed blond hair or wearing blond wigs.

All in all, the Ephesus that Mary suddenly found herself living in was a happy and civilized place. This was due in part to its wealth and in part to a city government that was enlightened even by modern standards. There was a fair tax system, and where it was unfair it favored the poor. For instance, there was a standard tax of one denarius on the issuing of a birth certificate, but if the mother was a

member of the upper class, or wished to be considered so, the tax was 100 denarii. Likewise, the poor were entitled to receive child benefits as well as free wheat and free entry to the public baths. The city's administrative council, the Demos, held its meetings in the Grand Theatre, where all Ephesians were free to attend. The Grand Theatre was also the venue for frequent musical concerts, poetry recitals, and the performance of classical plays. Ephesians of the first century were among the luckiest people in the Empire, and they knew it.

Nor was there anything to disturb their contentment – some would say smugness – until 53 AD when St Paul arrived on the scene to let them know that their gods had become superannuated: there was now only one God. At first he preached in the synagogues, but after a few months he moved to the lecture hall of Tyrannus where for two and a half years he taught every day from eleven to four in the afternoon. During this time he gained enough converts to cause more than a ripple

The Grand Theatre seen from Harbor Street

of anxiety, especially among the silversmiths whose livelihood depended in large part on the market for statues and medallions of Artemis.

One of these, the silversmith Demetrius, finally decided to do something about this threat to their lucrative trade, and so called a meeting of all those who made a living out of Artemis and other Greco-Roman deities. Once he had successfully inflamed his listeners with fears for their business, he then fanned the flames by insisting that this Christian interloper was also insulting the dignity of the great goddess herself. In their collective fury, his audience swelled into a mob that stormed the Grand Theatre, where for two hours they chanted "Great is Artemis of the Ephesians". As the contagion of group rage spread, the theatre filled with people who had only the dimmest idea why they were so enraged. Thus, not for the last time, commercial self-interest and shameless rabble-rousing had dovetailed neatly to create a monster of "popular opinion".

St Paul himself was eager to confront the crowd, to deal with their

St John and St Paul as depicted in a seventeenth-century English "Lives of the Apostles"

anger in person, but his friends persuaded him otherwise. As it was, with their help he just barely escaped with his life. In the end, order was restored only after the secretary to the city council appeared and reminded the crowd that if anyone had a complaint then the courts were the proper place to seek redress. Not long afterwards St Paul left Ephesus and went to Macedonia. In 64 AD he was martyred in Rome, and St John became head of the Church in Ephesus.

But theirs was by no means the only influential Christian presence in Ephesus during the early days of the Church. St Luke is known to have been there at one stage; some historians believe that he wrote his Gospel there. St Mark is reported to have accompanied St Peter there, and St Philip spent some time there before settling in Hierapolis, about 150 kilometers to the east, where he preached until his martyrdom.

How much of this missionary activity came to Mary's attention, or indeed how much of it she lived to see, is anybody's guess. As she is thought to have moved to the house on Nightingale Mountain within months of her arrival in Ephesus, she would have been remote from the everyday currents of news that coursed through the metropolis below. On the other hand, the members of the rapidly growing Christian community there, quite a few of whom were living nearby on the mountainside, would certainly have kept her in touch with events, while St John himself would have brought news of his apostolic journeys on behalf of the new religion.

Likewise, one can only speculate as to how long she lived in the house. Some put her death as early as 43 AD, others as late as 63 AD. My own guess is that it probably occurred sometime midway between those two dates. We will never know, just as we will never know the exact date of the Crucifixion. What matters is that, thanks to the curiosity and perseverance of some remarkable men and women many centuries later, we now know much more than we ever did about the years before her death, and I am convinced that we will learn still more in the future.

Chapter two

The Silting-up of History

Whatever the precise date of Mary's death, it came at a crucial moment for both Ephesus and the Church. Ephesus, on the one hand, was about to enter its Golden Age. From the middle of the first century until the end of the second century AD the city blossomed in petals of marble: temples, theatres, schools, stadiums, fountains, baths, ever more opulent villas, streets, ceremonial gates, and the magnificent Library of Celsus were all built during this period. By contrast, the Church, beginning with the martyrdom of St Paul and St Peter in 64 and 67 AD respectively, was about to undergo a long night of struggle and persecution.

Yet the future was neither as bright for Ephesus nor as grim for the Church as it might have appeared at the time. Ephesus, for all the exuberance of its public building works, had still not solved the centuries-old problem of the silting-up of its harbor. In 61 AD the municipal authorities made a determined effort to dredge the harbor, but silt from the River Cayster continued to threaten to cut the city off from the sea, and thus from the principal source of its wealth. When the Emperor Hadrian visited the city in 129 AD he gave his enthusiastic support to a massive harbor-cleaning project, but the Ephesians were fighting a battle they were destined to lose. Meanwhile, out of sight, Christianity was quietly taking root and spreading. By the

Death of the Virgin by Caravaggio

time of St John's death there were already twenty churches recorded in Ephesus and Asia Minor, and there was a significant body of Christian Scripture with which to inspire the faithful and educate the heathen.

Nor was silt the only threat to the prosperity of Ephesus. There was also an invisible enemy: inflation. When Nero died in 68 AD the amount of silver in the denarius had already been reduced to 74% from 94% in the reign of Augustus, and the coin had lost half a gram in weight. This combination of a slowly disappearing harbor and a rapidly devaluing currency would no doubt have eventually strangled Ephesus in any event, but in 262 AD the city was dealt a blow from which it never really recovered. A fleet of 500 ships, assembled by the Goths in Crimea, sailed down the Bosphorus and attacked the city, plundering it and destroying the Temple of Artemis. A century later, in 365 and 368 AD, two devastating earthquakes finally brought to a close Ephesus' days of Roman power and architectural glory.

Even before these terminal calamities, however, Ephesus had begun to resurrect itself, quite legitimately, as the Cradle of Christianity. After the Edict of Milan in 313 AD bestowed official toleration on the Church, the ancient Museion, the largest building in Ephesus, was converted into a church and dedicated to the Virgin Mary. (By this time there were 165 Christian churches recorded in Ephesus and Asia Minor, compared with 77 in Italy and 24 in the Holy Land.) And then a great basilica was built over the tomb of St John on the hill of Ayasoluk just north of Ephesus. When in 381 AD Christianity became the official religion of the Roman Empire, Ephesus was well on its way to becoming recognized as the birthplace of Christianity as well as the deathplace of Christ's Mother.

The recognition came in the summer of 431 AD, almost exactly four centuries after the Crucifixion, when ecclesiastical authorities decided to hold the Third Ecumenical Council in Ephesus at the Church of the Virgin Mary. Here the Council Fathers formalized the doctrine of *Theotokos*, Greek for "God-bearer", in which Mary was officially proclaimed to be the Mother of God. To underline further the point of

Virgin and Child by Tomaso de Modena

ΜΡ

choosing Ephesus as the place to confirm Mary's divine maternity, at the end of the Council the assembled bishops sent a letter to the clergy which pointed out that Ephesus was "the place where John the Theologian and the Blessed Virgin Mary, Mother of God, were."

It seems strange, then, and a little sad, that the Council Fathers, convened within sight of the house on Nightingale Mountain, failed to take advantage of a unique opportunity to investigate the nearby evidence of Mary's existence locally, and to hear the testimony of the devout Christian community in Ephesus, who maintained an illuminating oral tradition. But they were too preoccupied with theological matters to be distracted by such mundane considerations. In their eagerness to secure Mary's place in Heaven, they were happy to ignore the fact that

Above, Death of the Virgin. Mosaic from St Savior in Chora, Istanbul
Left, the Virgin from the Deesis mosaic, St Savior in Chora, Istanbul

their sacred work was being carried out in Mary's old neighborhood. And when they left, they took the newly-crowned Mother of God with them, to continue her life in icons, statues, prayers, candle flames, church bells, and the rose windows of great cathedrals.

The Christians of Ephesus might as well have put up a sign saying, "Mary doesn't live here anymore."

From then on it was always St John who was associated with Ephesus. In the sixth century the Emperor Justinian had a vast basilica built over St John's tomb and the earlier fourth-century basilica. More than 157 meters long and 78 meters wide, with six cupolas 35 meters high, the church covered the entire hilltop of Ayasoluk. Only St Sophia

Above, rose window depicting Mary's death, Chartres Cathedral
Right, Albrecht Dürer's woodcut of the Assumption

1510

in Constantinople, completed in 532 AD, rivaled it in magnificence. (Fittingly, much of the marble used in its construction came from the demolition of the Stadium in Ephesus, where once Christians had been tortured to death.) By this time, however, the silting-up of the harbor had turned it into a malarial swamp, with the result that almost all of the remaining population of Ephesus had left and moved to the higher ground surrounding Ayasoluk hill.

So, just as Ephesus' connection with the sea had finally been severed by the silt of the River Cayster, Mary's historical connection with Ephesus had finally disappeared under the silt of centuries. When St Gregory of Tours, writing in the sixth century, referred explicitly to the house "at the summit of a mountain near Ephesus [which had] four walls without a roof", he added only that "John lived there." And a century later St Willibald, the Bishop of Eichstadt, made a pilgrimage to Ephesus where, he wrote, he went up the mountain to the house "where St John the Evangelist used to pray." Mary's house had become John's house.

Mary was further separated from her corporeal past by the celebration, beginning in the seventh century, of the Feast of the Assumption on the 15th of August. Then, in the ninth century, Pope

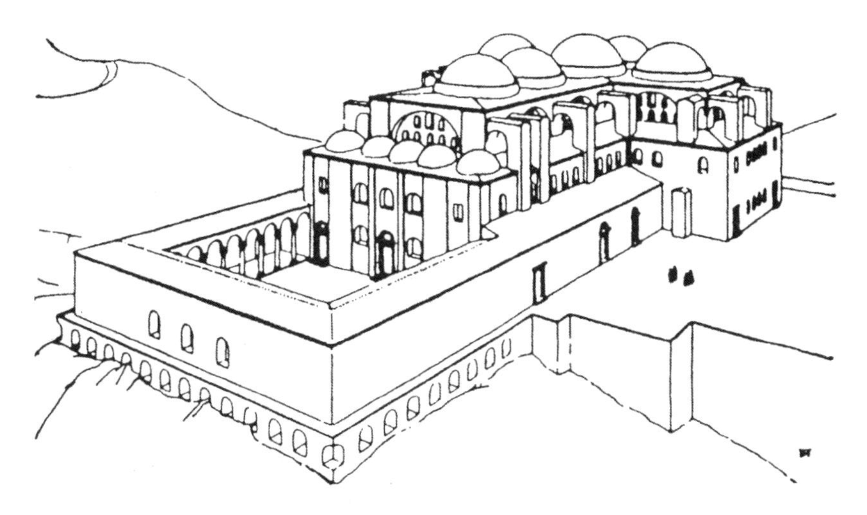

Artist's impression of St John's Basilica

The Ascension. Miniature from a collection of Homilies on the Virgin by James of Kokkinobaphus

Leo IV (847-855 AD) awarded the feast day a vigil before it and an octave afterwards, thereby solemnizing it above other feast days. Finally, Pope Nicholas I (858-867 AD) placed the Assumption on the same level as Christmas and Easter, thus implicitly decreeing that Mary's translation to Heaven ranked in importance with the birth and the resurrection of Christ. Accordingly, Mary came to be depicted in Byzantine art as celestial royalty, the enthroned and sceptred Queen of Heaven. Across Europe great churches were dedicated to her, and the bells of the Angelus, which had become the standard invocation to her, could be heard from the British Isles to the Middle East. Truly, by the end of the first millennium she had traveled a long way from the little house on Nightingale Mountain.

At the start of the second millennium Christianity had conquered all of Greece, Italy, France, Spain, the British Isles, Germany, Poland, Bohemia, Moravia, Serbia, Bulgaria, and Russia. But the opening century of the new millennium also saw the rise of a new threat to the Church's position in the East: the Seljuk Turks, who had rampaged into Asia Minor, routing the Byzantine army in 1071 at Manzikert, near Lake Van in eastern Turkey. Within a few years the Seljuks had reached the Aegean coast, causing the Ephesian Christians, to take one very important example, to flee into the mountains where they founded the Christian village of Kirinca.

Partly in response to this new threat, and partly as a result of the Church's continuing frustration at seeing Jerusalem under the sway of Islam, Pope Urban II in 1095 issued a call for Christians to go to the Holy Land and fight for the liberation of Jerusalem. To say that the idea caught on would be something of an understatement. The next year saw the launch of the First Crusade, and with it two centuries of pointless bloodshed in which the Church Militant returned to its roots with a vengeance.

Not least among the many ironies attending the Crusades was that they were undertaken under the spiritual patronage of the Blessed Virgin, against a foe whose holy book, the Koran, gives Mary much

The Assumption of The Virgin by El Greco

greater prominence and respect than is to be found in the Bible. In fact, Mary is mentioned no fewer than 34 times in the Koran, and is referred to as the only woman in the world not touched by Satan. Not only that, the Koran had confirmed that the birth of Jesus was the result of an Immaculate Conception – in other words, that the Virgin Mary was indeed a virgin, a concept with which Christian theologians were still struggling.

And for real connoisseurs of irony, there can be no doubting that the greatest crime against Christianity during the Crusades was committed not by the Islamic infidels but by the Crusaders themselves when they sacked Constantinople in 1205, pillaging the Christian churches, smashing the Christian icons, and putting the Christian citizens to the sword. Then they turned round and headed home! They got as far as Adrianople, where the Bulgars were waiting for them. They were annihilated, but they had succeeded in destroying the home of Eastern Christianity forever.

Nor, apparently, were any lessons learned from this debacle, for the very next Crusade was the Children's Crusade of 1212, in which the devout young of Europe were shepherded into Asia Minor to die of disease or to be sold into slavery. Yet still these ludicrous, murderous expeditions continued until the end of the century, by which time the Church was concentrating on heresies closer to Rome.

It was also at the end of this century that Mary began to undergo a transformation in Western art. She came to be portrayed as less distantly regal and more human, with more natural gestures and expressions. The real turning point probably came with the exquisite frescoes executed by Giotto in the church of S. Maria dell' Arena in Padua during the first decade of the fourteenth century. His approach was then picked up by the painters of the Florentine school, whereupon, over the next two centuries, the Mother of God reclaimed her other role as the mother of Jesus, while custody of her image passed into the hands of the great masters of the Renaissance: Fra Angelico, Botticelli, Ghirlandaio, Perugino, Piero della Francesca,

Detail of The Assumption by Titian

Mantegna, Dürer, Holbein, Bellini, Lippi, Lucas Cranach, Giorgione, Raphael, Leonardo, Michelangelo, and Titian, among others. Among *many* others: by the end of the sixteenth century Mary was easily the most widely depicted figure in the art of the Western world, if not of the whole world. At the same time she had become the focus of devotion and adoration in the colossal Gothic cathedrals that now dominated the landscape of Europe, those soaring hymns in stone to the glory of the True Faith, where homage to the Virgin echoed off the towering vaulted ceilings, especially after 1568, when the *Ave Maria* assumed a permanent place in the Roman Catholic breviary.

The Flight into Egypt by Giotto in the church of S. Maria dell' Arena in Padua

But what of the Ephesian Mary, the quiet, elderly lady who lived out her days in surroundings so humble that they had seemingly been forgotten altogether? As a matter of fact, despite the combined if unintended efforts of theologians and artists alike, neither she nor Ephesus had been completely forgotten. In 1650 the Franciscan monk Francesco Quaresimi wrote that when St John "left to preach the Gospel in Asia Minor he took the Holy Mother of God with him to live in Ephesus." And shortly thereafter the French ecclesiastical historian Louis de Tillemont wrote: "We do not see that there is any doubt that Mary lived in Ephesus and in fact that she died there." In the next century Pope Benedict XIV (1740-58) stated the case more emphatically, announcing flatly that "the Blessed Mary left this life in Ephesus and ascended into Heaven."

Voices such as these would probably have continued to be heard, growing fainter and further apart, until both the metaphorical and literal sands of time had finally buried the last traces of the earthly Mary, had it not been for another voice, from the unlikeliest source imaginable, that was about to speak up and put an end forever to Mary's exile in the far recesses of history.

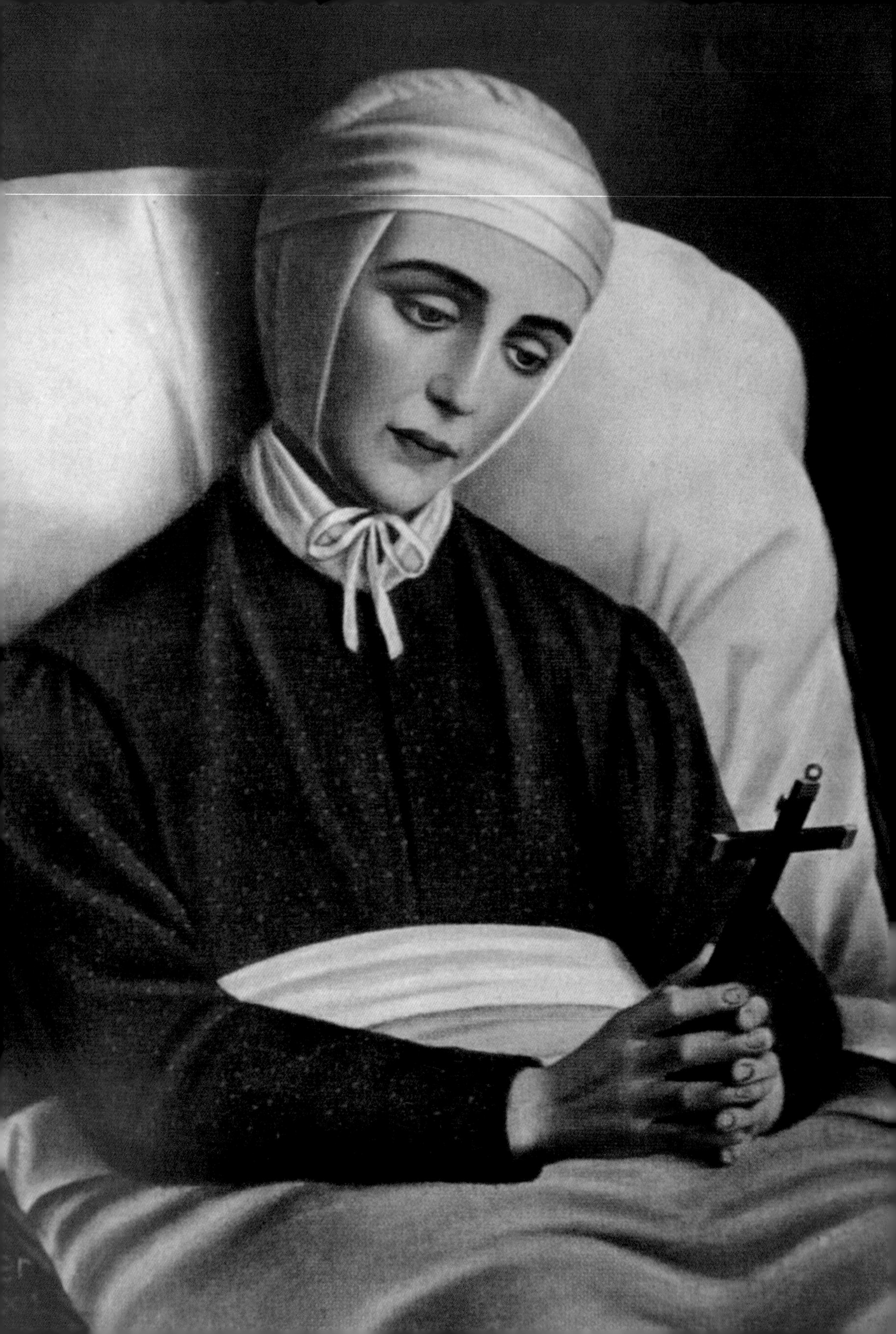

Chapter three

The Visions of Sister Emmerich

By the end of the eighteenth century the entire continent of Europe was convulsed by the shock waves produced by the French Revolution. Thomas Carlyle called it "the frightfullest thing ever born of Time", and certainly fright was its most obvious by-product, as the Jacobin Terror unleashed a frenzy of bloodletting. At first it was only the nobility and assorted courtiers who packed the tumbrils that clattered towards the scaffold past baying mobs, which were only momentarily hushed by the metallic whisper of the guillotine's blade before erupting again in vengeful delirium. But as the Terror began to feed on itself, so too did the baskets begin to fill with the severed heads of revolutionaries as well as counter-revolutionaries. By 1794 the Revolution had decapitated itself.

Before doing so, however, it loosed the hounds of hate to romp snarling into every corner of Europe, pursuing everyone and everything remotely associated with the *Ancien Régime*. This meant, of course, that the Church and the clergy were bound to be among the first to be targeted. But it still doesn't explain why the anti-ecclesiastical fury of the Jacobins came to be focused so strongly, so venomously, on the Virgin Mary herself. Images of Mary were removed from churches and burned, statues of her were broken into little pieces, including the famous Black Madonnas in the crypts of Mont St-Michel and Chartres. Crowds in the streets took

Sister Anne Catherine Emmerich

sacrilegious delight in invoking Marianne, the symbolic personification of the French Republic, as a substitute for Mary in their raucous prayers: "Virgin of Liberty, deliver us from Kings and Popes! Virgin of Equality, deliver us from aristocrats!" And in a particularly tasteless parody of the *Ave Maria*, they chanted, "Hail Marianne, full of strength, the People are with thee, Blessed is the fruit of thy womb, the Republic."

Napoleon's concordat with Pope Pius VII in 1801 put an end to the worst excesses of the Revolution, but even after Napoleonic dreams of Empire had long since overridden the more nightmarish Republican fantasies, the toxic fall-out from the Terror continued to poison the climate in which religious communities were forced to operate throughout Europe.

One such was the Augustinian cloister at Dülmen, a little country town southwest of Münster. In 1812 all of the monasteries and convents in western Germany were closed down, which meant that the nuns of Dülmen had to survive on the charity of those of the faithful who could take them into their homes. Perhaps the most difficult of these to place was Sister Anne Catherine Emmerich, a 38-year-old nun in such poor health that she had been virtually confined to her bed for years. Eventually, though, a room was found for her in a nearby house. She would not leave this room until her death twelve years later, by which time the room was almost constantly under devout siege by people of every station in life, aristocrats and peasants, prelates and laymen, the lettered and unlettered, rich and poor, young and old, many of whom had traveled great distances just to be in her presence. All because on the night of 29 December 1812 – while the last remnants of Napoleon's *Grande Armée* were still straggling back into France, leaving the snows of Russia stained with the blood of half a million men – Sister Emmerich suddenly began to bleed from her hands and feet.

She also began to have the visions that 80 years later would lead to the house on Nightingale Mountain.

The daughter of poor farm laborers, Anne Catherine Emmerich was born on 8 September 1774. Even as a very young girl she demonstrated the two characteristics that were to distinguish her adult life: chronically fragile health and cast-iron belief. Although work on

the farm exhausted her, she nonetheless found the strength regularly to complete the long and demanding Way of the Cross that had been re-created outside the town. And when her labors in the fields finally began to threaten her health, she went to work as a seamstress, where she impressed everyone with her ability to make dresses and make prayers simultaneously. She never went to school.

As she grew older, her piety hardened into a determination to enter a convent, but she was refused admission time and again because she could never come up with the small amount of money required for a nun's dowry. She gave away everything she earned as a seamstress, and the convents were too impoverished themselves to take on added financial burdens. But this only deepened her resolve to consecrate her life to the Church. Then at the age of 24 she began to experience sufferings that replicated those of Jesus in His final hours, including wounds to her forehead left by an unseen Crown of Thorns. Finally, at the age of 28, her head covered by lesions of unknown origin, she was admitted to the

French revolutionaries with looted church vestments and trappings

small Augustinian convent at Dülmen, where she lived until the suppression of the religious communities in 1812. Then, shortly after Christmas 1812, came the night when her stigmata appeared.

Those who were present on that night reported that as she prayed her face became flushed and she was apparently seized by a high fever. Then all of a sudden she was suffused by a brightness that specifically illuminated her hands and feet, which were seen to be covered with blood, as if they had been punctured. Likewise, a bleeding wound appeared on her side. Onlookers, understandably panicked, immediately sent for a doctor, but her condition was beyond the capacity of medical science to diagnose. There followed two lengthy investigations, one by an ecclesiastical commission and one by a civil commission, and both reported that as far as they could determine the stigmata were absolutely genuine.

For the remaining twelve years of her life Sister Emmerich was bedridden, in constant pain, bleeding into her bandages, and having visions of such intensity and vividness that they began to attract the attention of people far beyond the diocese of Münster. One of these was Clemens von Brentano, the German Romantic poet, who went to her bedside in 1818 and remained there off and on until her death in 1824, transcribing her accounts of her visions. When these transcriptions were finally published half a century later, it wasn't long before searchers and researchers were closing in on what the Turks call Meryemana Evi, the House of Mother Mary.

The visions, as recorded by Brentano, occupy several volumes and are mostly concerned with events from the life of Christ and of Mary. Only a few are devoted to Mary's final days in Ephesus, and those few follow no logical or even chronological sequence, tending to be circular rather than linear, creating and then clarifying ambiguities, so that in the highly condensed version that follows I have taken the liberty of reorganizing and summarizing Sister Emmerich's visions to help the reader see more clearly exactly what she saw.

Clemens von Brentano

THE LOCATION OF THE HOUSE

Mary did not live in Ephesus itself, but on a hill to the left of the road from Jerusalem… Narrow paths from Ephesus lead southwards to it… It is a very lonely place, but has many fertile slopes as well as rock caves where several Christian families and friends of Mary already lived… John had a house built for her here… It is on an uneven plateau near the top of the hill, overgrown with trees and wild bushes… There were Jewish as well as Christian settlers here, living in caves fitted out with woodwork or in huts or tents… It was like a scattered village… Mary's house was the only one built of stone… A little way behind it was the summit of the hill, from which one could see Ephesus and also the sea with its many islands… Near here is a castle inhabited by a king who seems to have been deposed…

Behind the house Mary had built a Way of the Cross soon after her arrival… It had twelve Stations… Mary paced out the measurements herself… At each Station she set up memorial stones – eight smooth stones with many sides, each resting on a base of the same stone… The stones and their bases were all inscribed with Hebrew letters… These Stations were all in little hollows, except the Station of Mount Calvary which was on a hill… The Station of the Holy Sepulchre was in a little cave over this hill…

THE HOUSE ITSELF

It was built of regular stones, rounded at the back, and had a spring running under it… The windows were high up near the flat roof… The main part of the house was divided into two by the fireplace in the middle of it, sunk into the ground, facing the door… There was a deep channel in the wall, like half of a chimney, which carried the smoke up to an opening in the ceiling… Behind the fireplace, the apse of the room was curtained off and formed Mary's oratory… In a niche in the centre of the wall there was a receptacle like a tabernacle and in it stood a cross about the length of a man's arm…

To the right and left of the fireplace were doors which led into the back part of the house… The door to the right led to the bedchamber of the Blessed Virgin, which ended in a semi-circle… Her couch, which was placed against a niche in the wall, was the length and breadth of a narrow plank… Through the door to the left of the oratory was a small room were Mary's clothes and other belongings were kept… She lived here quietly with her maidservant, a younger woman who fetched what little food they needed… John would visit them when he was not away on his travels…

MARY'S DEATH AND BURIAL

I saw her lying on a low, very narrow couch in her little sleeping alcove... Her head rested on a round cushion... She was very weak and pale... The assembled Apostles held a service in the front part of the house... Peter stood in priestly vestments before the altar, with the others behind him as if in a choir... I saw the Blessed Virgin being lifted up several times a day by the women to be given a spoonful of juice which had been pressed from a bunch of yellow berries... Newcomers tenderly embraced those who were already there... After their feet had been washed, they approached Mary's couch and greeted her with reverence... She could only say a few words to them... Towards evening she realized that her end was approaching and said farewell to the Apostles, disciples and women who were present... She lay back on her pillow, pale and still... Peter gave her Holy Communion... She died after the ninth hour, at the same time as Our Lord...

Matthew and Andrew then followed Mary's Way of the Cross until the last Station, half an hour's journey from the house, which was the cave representing the Holy Sepulchre... Here they worked to enlarge the tomb and to build a door with which to close the entrance... Women came to the house to prepare the body for burial, bringing with them cloths as well as spices to embalm the body... The house

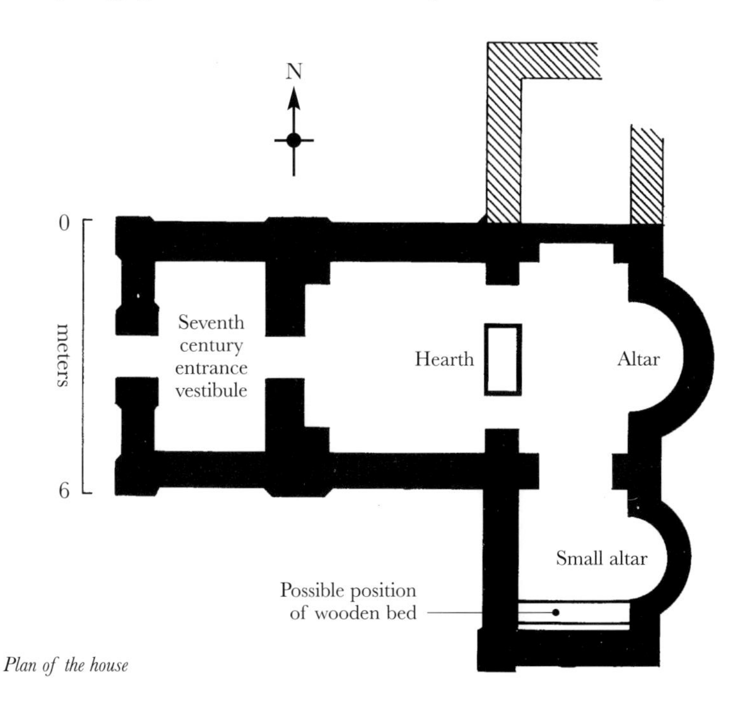

Plan of the house

was closed and they worked by lamplight… Two women washed the holy body… John carried a vessel with ointment… Peter dipped a finger of his right hand into it and anointed the breast, hands, and feet of the Blessed Virgin, praying as he did so… Bunches of myrrh were laid in the armpits and bosom and in the spaces between the shoulders and the neck, chin and cheeks… They wrapped the holy body in a great grave-cloth and placed it in the wicker coffin which stood near… On her breast was laid a wreath of red, white and sky-blue flowers… The coffin was then taken to the cave where she was buried…

On the question of the actual date of Mary's death, Sister Emmerich isn't much help. Or, rather, she is too much help: she offers all sorts of numbers (years in Ephesus, age at death, years Mary outlived Jesus *etc.*) but none of them makes sense when compared to what we know or can reasonably infer. To be fair, Sister Emmerich herself doesn't always appear to have much faith in her abstract numbers, pointing out that they have appeared in her visions as Roman numerals without any clear indication as to their significance.

In any case, the date of Mary's death perhaps fades in importance when Sister Emmerich tells us that after Mary's entombment St John took St Thomas, who had arrived late, to see the Virgin one last time. Once inside the cave, they knelt and St John opened the lid of the coffin. Mary's body was not in the burial shroud, but the shroud had remained intact. They carefully covered up the entrance to the cave and left.

Death of The Virgin by Hugo Van der Goes

Chapter four

"We have found it"

It would hardly be an exaggeration to say that when Clemens von Brentano's faithful accounts of Sister Emmerich's "revelations" were published, they aroused no detectable interest, nor did they for many years. In 1880, however, a copy of the Emmerich-Brentano *Life of the Holy Virgin* came into the hands of a French abbot, Father Julien Gouyet. Intrigued by the nun's claim to have seen Mary's house near Ephesus in her visions, Father Gouyet decided to go and look for it himself.

The following year he traveled to Smyrna, where he was warmly welcomed by the Archbishop, Monsignor André Timoni, who encouraged him in his quest and provided him with a young helper to accompany him. He also gave him, knowing the dangerous reputation of the mountains around Ephesus, a note in Greek which said, "Please spare this poor traveler, harmless and without resources." Happily, the note was not needed. Even more happily for Father Gouyet, he found the ruins of an ancient house which closely matched Sister Emmerich's description. On his return to Paris he wasted no time in informing both his diocesan superiors and the Vatican of this possibly momentous discovery. They, on the other hand, were quite happy to waste as much time as was necessary to discourage Father Gouyet from telling the

The house as it was discovered

outside world of this uncorroborated and potentially embarrassing "discovery" of his on a distant mountainside. At their subtle insistence, the matter was dropped.

And it stayed dropped for another decade, only to reappear in the strangest of circumstances. One day in mid-November 1890, Sister Marie de Mandat Grancey, the Mother Superior of the Sisters of Charity who ran the French Hospital in Smyrna, asked a visiting priest if he would give a reading from a book of his choice in the refectory after dinner that evening. The priest, Father Poulin, agreed and went to the library to select possible candidates for such a reading. Upon returning to his room, however, he was shocked and disgusted to find that somehow, inexplicably, among the books he had brought back was *The Life and Dolorous Passion of Our Lord Jesus Christ According to the Visions of Catherine Emmerich.*

Monsignor André Timoni

To understand his reaction, it is necessary to know that Eugène Poulin, a Lazarist Father, was also the Director of the French Sacred Heart College in Smyrna and a rigorous classical scholar who was deeply opposed to any form of mysticism. Nonetheless, he flipped though the Emmerich book until he found himself, to his surprise, reading it with greater and greater interest. Finally he decided to go ahead and try it out on his fellow priests at the hospital. It at once provoked a lively debate as to its significance, with most of the listeners expressing varying degrees of skepticism about the worth of such visions. The readings, and the debate, went on for more than a month. Then one evening in late December Father Poulin was approached by one of the older priests at the hospital, Father Dubulle, who asked whether he had read Sister Emmerich's *Life of the Holy Virgin.* No, he said, he hadn't known of its existence. Father Dubulle gave him a copy.

Sister Marie de Mandat Grancey

Readings from this book, with its descriptions of Mary's house and of her death and burial at Ephesus, ignited even more controversy than had the first book. Again, the skeptics were in the majority. Of these, the most outspoken in his denunciation of Sister Emmerich's visions was the hospital chaplain, Father Jung, a distinguished Hebrew scholar as well as Professor of Science at the Sacred Heart College. A determined enemy of mystics and visionaries, he ridiculed the visions as "girlish daydreams". Eventually, to resolve the issue it was suggested that a group of them should go to Ephesus during the summer holidays to try to establish the truth. This was unanimously agreed, and in a moment of inspired mischievousness it was further agreed that Father Jung should lead the expedition.

The group set out from Smyrna on Monday morning, 27 July 1891, and took the train to Ayasoluk (now Selçuk), the nearest stop to Ephesus. In the party were Father Jung, the still-unenthusiastic leader of the expedition; Father Benjamin Vervault, a Lazarist from the island of Santorini who had been visiting Smyrna and was almost as dismissive of mystical "truths" as Father Jung himself; a Greek friend of Father Jung's named Pelecas who had once been the station master at Ayasoluk and knew the Ephesus area well; and Thomaso, a Persian who worked at the Sacred Heart College and whose job it would be to take care of the luggage. At Ayasoluk they were joined by a fifth member of the team, a black Turkish Muslim named Mustafa who was hired to act as a combination mountain guide and bodyguard.

After spending all of Monday morning inspecting the ruins at Ephesus, they returned to Ayasoluk to eat and plan the next day's moves. These moves were to be complicated by the fact that back in February, on a visit to nearby Aydin, Father Poulin had met a Father Phillippe Pasel, who had himself undertaken a search for Mary's house and claimed to have found it at Dermen-Dérési, near Azizié (now Çamlik), further to the south. So they decided to take the train to Azizié early the next morning and proceed on foot from there. One can only assume that they reached this decision without reference to either Sister Emmerich or a railway timetable: whereas the nun spoke of narrow paths to the house from Ephesus, a timetable would have shown an

hour-long train journey before they could even begin to look for a path.

By 4.30 the next morning everybody was up and ready to go. After a small breakfast they polished their weapons – they had brought a small arsenal with them, including four rifles and five revolvers, to protect themselves against the bandits who notoriously roamed the mountains around here – and then left for the train station. At six they boarded a southbound goods train; by seven they were in Azizié. Finding a narrow path headed in the right direction, they took it. They

Father Eugène Poulin

trudged along for two and a half hours, whereupon they came upon a village that seemed to be eerily deserted. While Mustafa went off to look for someone who might know how to find Dermen-Dérési, the others rested in the shade of a tree.

As they sat discussing their prospects of finding Dermen-Dérési, doors in the village creaked open and women peered out. Then a few children came out to play. Mustafa returned with a large red-bearded man who eyed them all suspiciously until the subject of money was raised, at which point he became more than happy to take them to Dermen-Dérési, and to help Thomaso with the bags. After two more hours and two more villages they reached Dermen-Dérési. Far from being on the mountaintop envisaged by Sister Emmerich, it was in a deep gorge, where the only house to be seen was not the ancient remains of a modest dwelling but a large Greek Orthodox monastery built on the bank of a river.

They were received cordially by the monks and invited to stay for lunch, which turned out to be, as Father Vervault later described it, "a Lucullan feast" consisting of rice soup, an onion dish, a plate of fresh fish, various cheeses, and generous helpings of wine. Over lunch Father Jung satisfied himself that there was no point in searching the area further, and proposed that they head straight for Scala-Nova (now Kuşadası), where they could get a horse-drawn carriage back to Ayasoluk. They left at three o'clock, having sent Thomaso on ahead with a donkey to carry their luggage, and began the long post-prandial trek to Scala-Nova in the scorching midsummer heat. At one point along the way Pelecas collapsed, which slowed them down, but they managed to reach Scala-Nova, exhausted, before six. After reviving themselves at a seaside café, they found a carriage and horses to take them to Ayasoluk, a journey of over two hours itself because the elderly horses and elderly carriage both had to be rested at intervals. It was very late, and they were very weary, by the time they arrived back at their inn in Ayasoluk.

The next morning, Wednesday the 29th of July, nobody was up early. Nor did anyone object when it was proposed that this time they should stick to Sister Emmerich's directions. After Father Jung had arranged for Mustafa to buy provisions and have them sent ahead to a little café near

the foot of Nightingale Mountain, they all set off on aching limbs to follow the old Jerusalem road south until it curled past the eastern edge of Ephesus, where they would leave the road and look for a path up into the mountains. It was over an hour before they found a usable path, by which time the sun was high in the sky. Scratched by the brambles that choked the little path, and drenched with sweat that glued their clothes to their skin, they made their way slowly up the mountain, pausing every so often to catch their breath and drink from their flasks of water. When the water ran out, Pelecas lay on the ground and declared that he would rather die than go any further. It was only with great difficulty that the others persuaded him to get up and continue.

Soon they came to a small plateau where some women were working in a tobacco field. Pelecas immediately began crying out, *"Nero!"* (Greek for water). The women said they had no water, but that there

Father MH Jung

was a spring just up the mountain "at the monastery". It took Father Jung and his thirsty band of men less than 15 minutes to find the spring and "the monastery", which was not much more than a small heap of rubble surrounded by crudely built shacks of various shapes and sizes. Somewhat surprisingly, these rickety structures appeared to be inhabited. After the new arrivals had refreshed themselves at the spring, some of the inhabitants emerged to extend a cautious welcome.

Foremost among these were Andreas and Yorgy, who became very friendly once they had established that the newcomers were not government officials of some kind. Andreas immediately offered to go off and get something for them to eat, while Yorgy chatted away amiably to Pelecas. Mustafa borrowed a horse to go and fetch the supplies that he had despatched earlier that morning. Father Jung, in the meantime, began to be curious about the little ruin that was the centerpiece of the encampment. After poking around among the stones, it suddenly dawned on him that the basic configuration of the ruin conformed almost exactly to Sister Emmerich's description of Mary's house. Could they have accidentally stumbled on the object of their search? Father Jung asked Yorgy if a little higher up it was possible to see both Ephesus *and* the sea. Yorgy said yes, that Bülbül Dağı was the only place where you could see both, and offered to show him. Father Vervault and Thomaso, realizing the significance of all this, eagerly joined Father Jung and Yorgy for the short climb. When they reached the top, there below them, to the north, was the plain of Ephesus, and to the west they could see the mountainous island of Samos, exactly as Sister Emmerich had said.

On the way back down to the house, Father Jung asked Yorgy if there were any tombs nearby. Oh yes, Yorgy said, very old tombs. Father Jung asked if by any chance he knew where the tomb of the Virgin Mary was. No, said Yorgy, but he could take him to the tomb of Mary Magdalene. Everybody knew where that was. One imagines that on hearing this the austere Father Jung permitted himself at least a hint of a smile.

Map of the area from Izmir to Çamlik

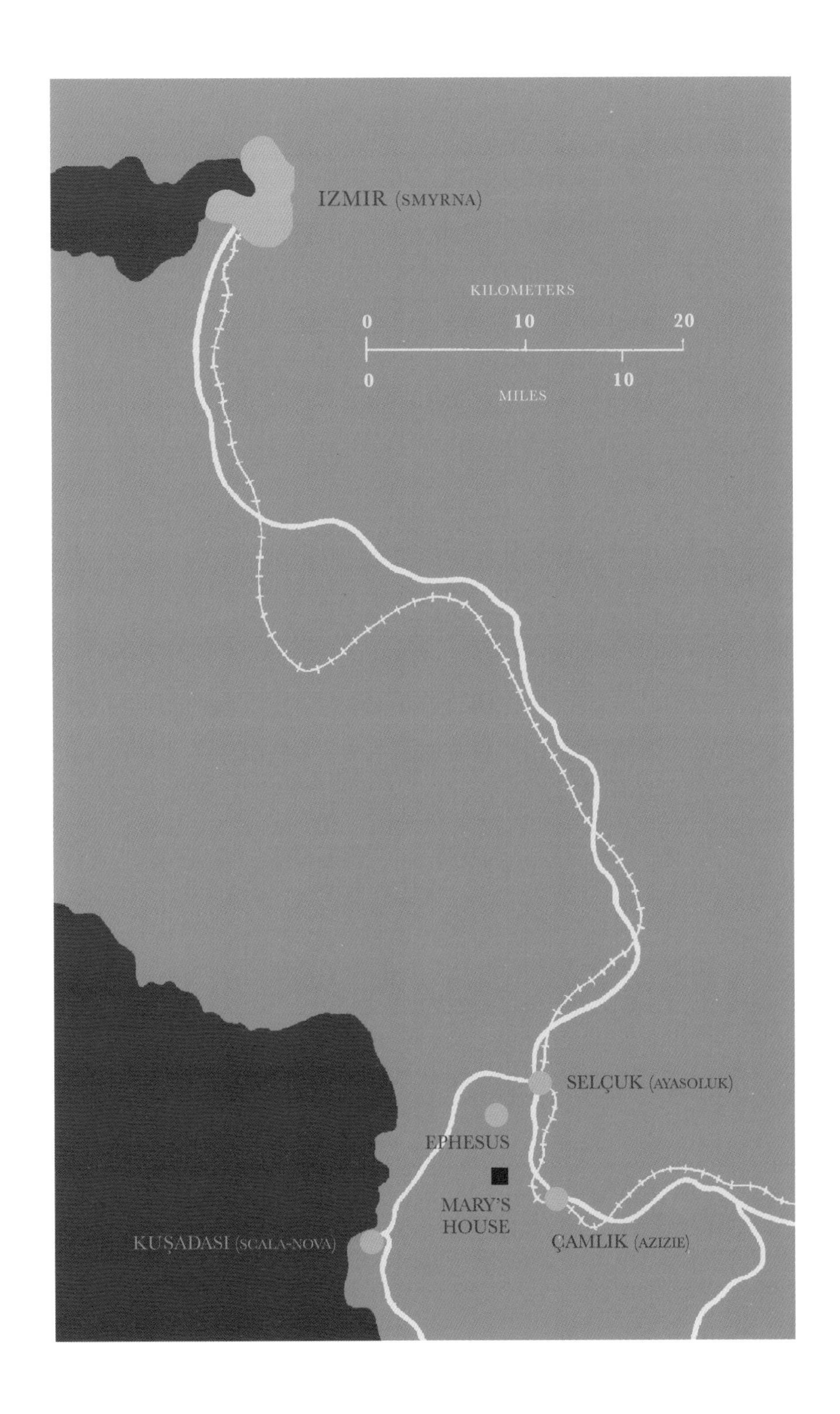
IZMIR (SMYRNA)
KILOMETERS
0
10
20
0
10
MILES
SELÇUK (AYASOLUK)
EPHESUS
MARY'S HOUSE
KUŞADASI (SCALA-NOVA)
ÇAMLIK (AZIZIE)

Shortly after they had got back downhill, where Pelecas was still resting from his morning's exertions, Andreas arrived with a large thigh of wild boar which was immediately put on the fire. Then Mustafa arrived with his provisions, expanding the picnic into a banquet. As they sat on the ground under a plane tree, feeding themselves with their fingers, Andreas explained that actually he had built all the wooden shelters they saw around them. One was for himself and his family, but they only lived there during the tobacco-growing season; he had a tobacco field not far way that he rented. Another hut was for Yorgy, his helper. The other, larger shacks were for storing crops, farm implements, and supplies, and in the winter for lodging animals. His actual home was in Kirinca, about five hours away in the mountains, where his Christian ancestors had fled from the invading Seljuk Turks many centuries ago.

After lunch Andreas laid out some straw mattresses under the trees so that they could all sleep off their meal, out of the worst of the mid-

The south side of the house as found

afternoon heat. At 5.30 Father Jung announced that it was time for his group to leave. Andreas offered his services as a guide, and his donkey's services as a beast of burden, on any further explorations they might be contemplating, an offer which was gratefully accepted. He then showed them a better path down the mountain, one that followed the wall of Lysimachus back to Ayasoluk.

There is no way of knowing what kind of thoughts were going through Father Jung's demanding, scientific mind that hot afternoon as they descended Nightingale Mountain for the first time, but a tantalizing clue is to be found in the journal kept by Benjamin Vervault. Father Vervault records that at one point in their descent they spotted a wolf on a rock paying careful attention to a herd of goats below. Suddenly and uncharacteristically, Father Jung grabbed his rifle and fired at the wolf. Then both he and the wolf continued what they were doing as if nothing had happened.

When the little search party reached their inn at Ayasoluk that

The house on the day of its discovery

evening, Father Vervault summed up the day's events in his journal with the no-nonsense eloquence born of triumph and fatigue: "We looked, and we have found it."

Sadly for posterity, Father Vervault had to leave for Smyrna the next day in order to be back in Santorini the following week. Father Jung headed off in the opposite direction – to Azizié and Dermen-Dérési to tell the monks of the discovery. It was not until the afternoon of the following day, Friday the 31st, that Father Jung and his companions returned to the scene of their find. This time they tried taking a new path, but it proved to be a bad idea. It was even more arduous than the one they had taken originally – so arduous, in fact, that Father Jung himself fainted within a few hundred meters of the house. Thomaso went and got some fresh water and after a few minutes managed to revive him. It was two o'clock when they reached the house.

Father Jung spent most of the afternoon studying the ruins, occasionally muttering to himself, and then later the overall site. He

The round cistern found lower down the mountain

remarked on the eight magnificent plane trees that surrounded the house, linked together over the roofless shell by venerable and impressive grapevines. In front of the house, but lower down the mountain on an area of level terracing, he discovered the remains of a round cistern. It was connected by means of a man-made channel to the corner of the house where the spring appeared. Most importantly, up behind the house he found rocks with Hebrew inscriptions. Sister Emmerich had claimed that there were Jewish settlers living on the mountainside prior to Mary's arrival, and that Mary herself had used stones inscribed with Hebrew letters in creating her own Way of the Cross: if hard evidence was needed, it didn't come any harder than this.

Less tangible, but no less important, evidence surfaced that evening. As the plan called for Father Jung and his men to spend the night on the mountain, their meal with Andreas and his family offered an excellent opportunity for Father Jung to tap into the oral history of the house. He learned, for example, that Andreas had been coming there for 30 years, and before that his father went there, and that the people of his village had *always* gone there to pray in memory of the Holy Virgin. Father Jung wanted to know if the place was known locally by any particular name. Yes, said Andreas, it was known as Panaghia-Capouli, "The Gate of the All Holy", to the people of his village. He added that they were the only people who ever dared to go there. Everyone else was scared away by the murderous brigands who infested the mountains.

At the end of another tiring but rewarding day, everyone slept well under the great canopy of plane trees – except for Thomaso, who sat up all night with his rifle across his lap, waiting for the slightest crunch of a villain's footsteps.

They spent Saturday morning on the mountain, so that Father Jung could make one more tour of inspection, and then caught the train back to Smyrna in the late afternoon. The next day Father Jung went to see Father Poulin to report on their trip. His report concluded with the opinion that they had indeed found the house where the Virgin Mary died. Father Poulin did not bother to conceal his shock on hearing this. Father Jung, of all people, the Voice of Reason, the diehard upholder of the scientific method, the scourge of mystics, was actually lending his support to the "girlish daydreams" he had once so fervently denounced?

In that case, Father Poulin announced, he had better go and see for himself this house which was causing so much commotion. Preferably sooner rather than later.

Father Jung took the hint. On Wednesday evening the 12th of August, the two scholar-priests met for an early meal at the French Hospital, and then retired to get a few hours' sleep before catching the goods train that left Smyrna shortly after midnight. At Sister Grancey's insistence they took with them the hospital's gardener, Constantin Grollot, who was said to be an excellent shot and could therefore wield his rifle in their defense. It was a miserable journey. There were no seats or benches in the van, the night was moonless and chilly, and they were constantly being jolted back and forth as the train stopped at every little station along the way. When they finally arrived, the early-morning trek up the mountain came almost as a welcome release.

Hardly had they arrived at the house before Father Poulin was examining the site and checking everything he found against the details provided by Sister Emmerich: the size and shape of the house, the arrangement of the rooms, the little stream, the rock formations up the hill behind the house, the view of the sea as well as Ephesus at the top. Little by little, detail by detail, his doubts began to drop away. But he still had questions. Where, for example, was the fireplace that divided the main room? Father Jung had him stand where Sister Emmerich had indicated it was, and then read out the relevant passages that would place other aspects of the house in relation to it; everything fit. But what had become of the second little room, opposite Mary's bedchamber? True, it was no longer there, but there were the remains of an archway that had to be the entrance to *something*. Finally, the little vestibule at the entrance to the house – why hadn't Sister Emmerich mentioned it? Impossible to say, but in the context both of the house and the vision it was certainly marginal.

That evening, back at the inn in Ayasoluk where they were to spend the night before returning to Smyrna, Father Poulin wasn't yet ready to say that he had left all of his doubts up on Nightingale Mountain, but he had left enough of them behind to know that they now had a sacred duty to look after whatever it was they *had* discovered.

As a consequence, Father Jung immediately organized a third expedition up the mountain. Unlike the previous ones, this one was to consist exclusively of laymen, apart from Father Jung himself, and they were to spend an entire week encamped on the mountainside, with the goal this time of leaving no stone unturned – nor, for that matter, undocumented, undrawn, unmeasured, or unphotographed. As far as Father Jung was concerned, this expedition would be decisive in determining whether the stones would henceforth be known as the remains of a "monastery", as first identified by the women working in the tobacco fields, or as part of "The Gate of the All Holy", as it was known to Andreas and the Christian villagers of Kirinca, or whether it was what Sister Emmerich had disturbingly predicted it was: the house where the Virgin Mary died.

P D'Andria's pen and ink drawing of the house, 1896

Their week-long endeavors produced, in addition to much precise documentation, two major successes. The first was the discovery, about 1200 meters from the house, of the ruins of a castle. Sister Emmerich had said there was a castle nearby. The second, serial success resulted from closer inspection of the presumed Stations of the Cross, which revealed each to be more carefully marked, and symmetrically bordered, than had been noticed previously. In particular, the highest Station was so meticulously formed, so impressively sited, that Father Jung was moved to baptize it in the name of the Station of Calvary. Their only disappointment was their failure to discover Mary's tomb.

On Sunday, 23 August 1891, the first Mass in Latin was said at the house. It was an appropriately homespun affair. Andreas had built a wobbly altar out of bits of wood he had scavenged. Then, assisted by Andreas and his wife and daughters, as well as by his lay companions, Father Jung said Mass. It so affected the Greeks present that they implored Father Jung to stay on until the 27th in order to say Mass for their own Feast of the Assumption. Unfortunately he had to be back in Smyrna on the 26th for the beginning of the Lazarists' annual retreat.

It had only been one month since that first skeptical search party had set off, rather reluctantly, on their holy treasure hunt, yet already the focus was beginning to shift from establishing the house's pedigree – a consensus was rapidly forming on that question – to finding a way to protect a property that was indeed a treasure.

The only sure way was to buy it. But there were huge obstacles on the way to this solution: the problem of finding the owner of the property, the problem of finding the money to buy it, and the problem of persuading the owner to sell it. The first of these problems was overcome with surprising ease, and with a dollop of good luck thrown in. On 27 January 1892, Fathers Poulin and Jung, together with a business-wise friend, Monsieur Binson of the Imperial Ottoman Tobacco Company, were traveling by train to Ayasoluk to make discreet enquiries about the ownership of the land around Ephesus when a young Greek entered their compartment. By a happy coincidence Binson knew the young man's employer; by an even happier coincidence the young man knew that the land in question was

jointly owned by the Bey of Arvaia, a very grand Turk, and his profligate nephew Ibrahim. Not only that, he also knew that both happened to be in need of money right now.

Wasting no time, the two priests and Binson made an appointment to see the Bey as soon as they arrived in Ayasoluk. He received them that afternoon. After an elaborate exchange of courtesies, and ritualized small talk lasting for hours, Binson, the only Turkish speaker among the three guests, brought up the subject of buying the Bey's land at Ephesus. The Bey said he would think about it. Joyfully, having solved one and a half of the three problems in a single trip, the visitors returned to Smyrna with the good news. There they were greeted with even more good news. Sister Grancey, who had believed in Mary's house from the very beginning, was prepared to put up her own private fortune to buy the property. Accordingly, on the 27th of February, she deposited 45,000 francs in the Smyrna branch of the Crédit Lyonnais bank, in a special account set aside for the purchase. Now it was just a matter of waiting for the Bey to make up his mind.

Father Jung and Sister Marie de Mandat Grancey at one of the Stations of the Cross

And waiting. For months the wily old Turk bobbed and weaved, employing every conceivable delaying tactic while he tried to bid the price up on the one hand and to look for alternative financing on the other. Several times the deal was on the brink of being completed, only for the Bey to withdraw at the last moment. Finally, on 15 November 1892, the waiting was over. It was Father Poulin's feast day, and as he was leaving Mass at 8.30 that morning he was handed a telegram. It read simply:

BONNE FETE. AFFAIRE TERMINEE. BINSON.

Binson had closed the deal the previous afternoon. The final sale price was 31,000 francs. The property, which comprised a total of 139 hectares, was roughly two kilometers in length and an average of one kilometer in width overall. It was registered in the name of Sister Marie de Mandat Grancey.

The delegation to the site led by Archbishop Timoni (center left)

Two weeks later, Father Poulin decided that the time had come to do something that he had been putting off for sixteen months. He went to Archbishop Timoni and told him of the discovery on Nightingale Mountain. Far from being dubious about this unexpected news, as Father Poulin had feared, the Archbishop was delighted by it. He said that he had thought all along that Mary had died in Ephesus. In fact, he was so excited about the news that he immediately announced his intention to lead an official delegation to the site. And the very next day he formed a commission of enquiry consisting of twelve dignitaries, seven Churchmen and five laymen, including Fathers Poulin and Jung, who would accompany him to Ephesus. A breathtaken Father Poulin was left to make all the necessary arrangements.

On Thursday morning the 1st of December Archbishop Timoni's delegation, plus Pelecas and Constantin Grollot, arrived at Ayasoluk station, where they were met by Binson, who had brought horses for them all. Andreas and Mustafa were on hand as well. The party then filed out of the station and headed for Sister Grancey's new property, arriving there about eleven o'clock. After hours spent examining the evidence and comparing it to Sister Emmerich's description of Mary's house and environs, and after much conferring among themselves, the dignified old prelate and his companions made the return journey to Smyrna. There Archbishop Timoni composed a lengthy document listing in detail their findings and showing how they conformed exactly to the descriptions found in Sister Emmerich's *Life of the Holy Virgin*. The document, which was signed by every member of the commission, concluded that "the ruins of Panaghia-Capouli are truly the remains of the house inhabited by the Virgin Mary."

At last, the Church had spoken.

Chapter five

Digging Deeper into the Past

With the house now in safe hands, the top priority was to make it more accessible by building a road up to it, however primitive. It was decided that the road should run more or less directly from Ayasoluk, cutting across the plain of Ephesus. Over 60 workers were recruited from nearby villages, and work on the road began almost immediately under the supervision of Contantin Grollot.

The next priority was to fix up the house itself without interfering with it. To this end they replaced the crumbling front door with a new and solid one; they installed a small metal gate at the outside entrance to the bedchamber, to keep out dogs and other animals; they removed the debris and a layer of earth that covered the floor; they applied judicious amounts of cement to the walls to prevent any further deterioration; they suspended a temporary roof over the whole structure to protect it and the workers from the elements; and they began planting the olive trees which now line the footpath leading to the house.

By the early summer of 1894 these preliminary tasks were largely completed. Then, after a long, frustrating series of refusals and delays, the Turkish authorities finally gave permission for the construction of other buildings on the site to provide permanent lodging for Andreas and his family, who would continue to live there both as workers and caretakers, and for visiting religious notables and pilgrims. At once the

The Temple of Domitian with Nightingale Mountain in the background

mountainside became a hive of activity, as men drove donkeys up from Ephesus laden with bricks and across the mountain with bits of limestone for the ovens, while masons and bricklayers toiled to erect the new houses and others labored to complete the road and lay paving stones for the terrace, all under the watchful eye of Constantin Grollot, who patrolled the site with a pickaxe in one hand and a rifle in the other. By mid-September the work was finished.

As a result of all this feverish industry, Grollot's men not only gave the site a completely new look but in the process unearthed some fascinating glimpses of its look centuries earlier. Of these the one that easily caused the most excitement occurred when the pickaxes of workers trying to level a bit of ground further up the hill repeatedly struck a large rock beneath the surface. The workers told Grollot they thought they might have found a tomb. Grollot immediately summoned Father Jung, who examined the stone and decided that it had most probably been put in place by hand. He asked the workers if they could dig elsewhere for a while, then with Grollot's help gently wrestled the stone aside. Underneath was the top of an underground wall. The workers were called back and asked to continue digging, carefully, along the line of the wall. They came upon two more walls, at right angles, and in the middle a huge earthenware jar that must have served as some kind of basin. Whatever they had discovered, an atrium perhaps, it was clearly not a tomb.

Compensating for this disappointment was a series of discoveries over the next few years which proved conclusively that for many centuries Mary's house had been a unique place of worship and veneration. To begin with, they discovered that the house had been restored several times, yet it had never been expanded or "improved". Every restoration had taken place strictly according to the original layout and on top of the original foundation: a clear indication that the building itself was regarded as sacrosanct. Confirming this was the discovery near the house of two terracotta sarcophagi, each containing a complete skeleton with the head pointed towards the house in a posthumous gesture of respect. Among the bones of one skeleton was a coin from the reign of Constans II (641-648 AD); alongside the other

they found a coin from the reign of Justinian II (685-695 AD).

Interestingly, these were by no means the earliest of the coins they unearthed. The earliest bore the head of Anastasius I, who reigned from 491-518 AD – or, in other words, from 60 years after the Third Ecumenical Council proclaimed Mary to be the Mother of God until about 40 years before the completion of the great basilica dedicated to St John. So while Mary's house may have escaped the notice of the princes of both the Roman Church and the Roman Empire, it remained important in the lives of ordinary and not so ordinary Christians around Ephesus.

And just who were these people who over hundreds of years had taken the trouble to preserve the house as a holy place? Obviously, the descendants of the early Christians who had lived on the mountainside would have felt it their duty to protect the house as best they could. But the evidence unearthed between 1894 and the winter of 1898-99 suggested the presence of a more formally religious community. From

The front of the house seen from the southwest

the vaulted arches, the columns, mosaics, burial urns (one containing the bones of an infant), the channels for the spring, glass and ceramic objects, vases, bronze coins, funerary lamps and other artefacts it was concluded that there must have been a monastery on the site. This conclusion was powerfully reinforced when it was learned that in ancient Ottoman land registers Mary's house was listed as "The Three-Doored Monastery of the All Holy". This would explain why the women in the tobacco field had referred to it as "the monastery",

Pope Leo XIII

and why the villagers of Kirinca called it Panaghia-Capouli, "The Gate of the All Holy".

These developments did not go unnoticed in the Vatican. In 1895 Pope Leo XIII sent Father Eschbach, the Superior of the French Pontifical Seminary in Rome, to Ephesus to meet with Father Jung and inspect the site. After Father Jung had escorted him around, he gave him some photographs which he himself had taken on the very day they discovered the house in July 1891. Father Eschbach took the pictures back with him to show the Pope, who was so moved by them that he kept them for himself. The following April he declared Mary's house a place of pilgrimage. Within a month over a thousand pilgrims had arrived at the site, while the French press excitedly, if somewhat belatedly, reported the discoveries on Nightingale Mountain.

But the most dramatic discovery of all was still to come.

On Thursday, 24 August 1898, at half past three in the afternoon, workers clearing away the earth in the main room of Mary's house suddenly came upon some blackened fragments of marble about 50 centimeters below the surface. Further digging revealed more blackened stones. As this was at the exact spot where Sister Emmerich had located the fireplace, work was halted until an expert could examine the stones. The next day an archaeologist from Smyrna, Professor Weber, arrived and undertook a careful analysis of the specimens they had uncovered. He announced that the blackening had definitely been caused by soot, and as it was so concentrated the only possible conclusion was that there had once been a fireplace there.

To those who had spent years rescuing Mary's house from oblivion, it was as if the fire at the heart of the house had never gone out.

Chapter six

The House Today

Given the momentous and auspicious events that marked the closing decade of the nineteenth century on Nightingale Mountain, one would have thought that Mary's house would enter the twentieth century on course for a smooth and swift elevation from neglected ruin to celebrated shrine. Moreover, it received an unexpected boost in this direction when in 1902 the first apparition of the Madonna was witnessed at the house, followed by the first reports of cures after drinking the water from the spring. Even the death in 1903 of Pope Leo XIII, a strong believer in the uniquely sacred character of Mary's house, didn't appear to damage its chances of worldwide recognition, because Leo's successor, Pope Pius X, was quick to send his congratulations and apostolic blessing to the Lazarist Fathers and to encourage them to continue their explorations. Indeed, in 1914 he granted a plenary indulgence for the remission of the sins of pilgrims to the shrine.

Within months, however, the house had become one of the first casualties of the Great War. It and all the land that Sister Grancey had bought were immediately confiscated by the Turkish government, not only because of the property's strategic location overlooking the Aegean, but also because Turkey had entered the war on the side of Germany and thus was now at war with the French. Nor did the defeat of the Central Powers in 1918 bring any change in the house's

The entrance to the house

situation. If anything, it suffered even more from the "peace" that followed, as the Greeks invaded at Smyrna and Mustafa Kemal (later Atatürk) launched his revolution against the Ottoman sultanate in Istanbul. For the next four years all of Turkey was in a state of violent upheaval. It was not until the end of 1922 that the revolution had triumphed, the sultanate had been abolished, and Mustafa Kemal's armies had defeated the Italian and French occupation forces and driven the Greeks (literally) back into the sea.

Then during the remainder of the Twenties the Turks were preoccupied with building a modern, secular, Kemalist republic. Not surprisingly, the preservation of a small Christian shrine on the country's west coast failed to make it on to anyone's agenda – except that of the Lazarist Fathers, who worked patiently to get the government to recognize their legal right to the property. (As Sister Grancey had signed over the property to Father Poulin in 1910, and

Mustafa Kemal Atatürk

Father Poulin died in 1928, the Lazarists eventually petitioned the court on their own behalf.) The issue was still unresolved in the summer of 1931 when Cardinal Angelo Roncalli, later Pope John XXIII, led a delegation to Ephesus to mark the fifteenth centenary of the Third Ecumenical Council in the Church of the Virgin Mary. Sadly, the roadway up the mountain had become virtually impassable in the four decades since it was built and so the delegation was prevented from visiting the house.

Finally, on 24 September 1931, the feast day of Our Lady of Ransom, the court ruled that the property did indeed belong to the Lazarists.

But where the Great War had effectively nullified the Pope's decree in 1914, now it was the Great Depression that condemned Mary's house to further deterioration and obscurity. And by the time the Depression was over, the world was at war again, though this time without Turkey's involvement, which meant that the little house

The delegation of 1931 led by Cardinal Roncalli, later Pope John XXIII, who stands second from the right

continued to languish in its wooded isolation above Ephesus, exiled from the world's attention. Even the end of the war didn't signal any change in this melancholy state of affairs, because everything in the eastern Mediterranean was soon overshadowed by the turmoil surrounding the creation of a Jewish state in Palestine in 1948.

The turning point for the house finally came on 1 November 1950, when Pope Pius XII issued his encyclical *Munificentissimus Deus* which proclaimed the dogma of the Assumption of Mary into Heaven. Although this merely incorporated into Church doctrine a long-held belief among Christians, its effect was immediate and dramatic. Suddenly people began to wonder, often for the first time, just where Mary had been assumed into Heaven *from*. They didn't have long to wonder. Within months the Pope had declared Mary's house an official shrine for pilgrims and confirmed the plenary indulgence for all pilgrimages there. He also decreed that visiting priests could celebrate the Votive Mass of the Assumption at the shrine. At last Nightingale Mountain was on the religious map.

Shortly afterwards the Archbishop of Izmir, the Most Reverend Joseph Descuffi, formed a local non-profit association to take care of the property and to begin the full-scale restoration of the house. Ownership as well as custodianship of the property was then handed over to the association. Meanwhile, the Turkish government began building a new paved road up the mountain and had electricity installed at the site. New buildings were constructed to house the caretakers and resident ecclesiastics, and new signs sprouted along the main road below pointing the way to the house of *Meryemana* (Mother Mary). It was not long before coachloads of pilgrims were following those signs.

Such was the newfound interest in Mary's house that a major discovery in 1952 was treated almost as a distant footnote to the monumental discoveries of the 1890s. A large sarcophagus was unearthed near the entrance of a grotto on the outskirts of Ephesus known as the Cave of the Seven Sleepers, so-called because of an

Part of the necropolis at the Cave of the Seven Sleepers

ancient Christian legend attached to it. The sarcophagus was positively identified by Professor Louis Massignon of the Collège de France as the tomb of Mary Magdalene. The bones were removed and are now in the Church of St Mary Magdalene in Paris.

Interest in the house, and pilgrimages to it, continued to grow throughout the Fifties, and were further stimulated when in 1960 Pope John XXIII sent a special candle to Mary's house on the feast day of the Purification of the Blessed Virgin, also known as Candlemas. These Candlemas candles are only sent to the most important Marian shrines in the world. To underline the point, the Pope then reconfirmed the plenary indulgence for pilgrims visiting the house.

A sarcophagus, similar to that of Mary Magdalene, in the Cave of the Seven Sleepers

The next significant date in the modern history of the house is 26 July 1967, the day that Pope Paul VI made the first papal visit to the house. The Pope arrived in the middle of the afternoon, looking frail and exhausted in the summer heat, and made his way through the crowd to the house, where he was joined inside by several priests. There he knelt in prayer. His prayers, beginning with the Angelus, were then broadcast to the people outside. Afterwards he presented a bronze lamp to Father Filibert de la Chaise, the Capuchin monk in charge of looking after the house. "This is a present for the Blessed Virgin," he said.

The next papal visit – by Pope John Paul II – occured on 30 November 1979, and was a much more public occasion. Like his predecessor, the Pope went straight to the house and spent some time in private prayer. Then he celebrated Mass outdoors before an altar that had been placed on a raised bank next to the house, while over 2,000 people jostled and craned to get a better view of the Holy Father.

Pope Paul VI praying before the altar in Mary's house

At the end of the Mass he distributed Communion himself to as many people as he reasonably could, and then addressed the pilgrims in French, Italian, English, and Polish. Finally, there was a presentation of gifts to the Pope, among which was a magnificent edition of the Koran presented by the Mayor of Selçuk, who said he was hoping to emphasize the fact that Muslims, too, revered Mary.

It was this visit that really brought the little shrine to the notice of the world at large. Ever since, it has been the destination for pilgrims from every geographical and doctrinal corner of Christendom, Protestant as well as Catholic. It is estimated that well over a million people a year make the journey to Mary's house. Some come for the reputed healing powers of the water (a reputation that would appear to be not without foundation, judging by the number of crutches and other limb supports that have collected there, as well as objects left

Pope John Paul II celebrating Mass outside the house

behind in thanksgiving). Others, Christians and Muslims alike, simply come to pray at a holy place. Still others come just out of curiosity, to see a spot where it is believed that the Virgin Mary spent her last years on earth. Whatever the reason for visiting the house, all visitors agree that, despite the crowds that throng the site in summer, it remains a place of uncommon serenity and sanctity.

At first sight, however, it appears no different from any other popular tourist attraction. The entrance to the site is lined with the usual shops and stalls selling souvenirs in doubtful taste mixed with religious bric-a-brac of often breathtaking vulgarity. But once inside the site the atmosphere changes at once. The palpable holiness of the surroundings silently enforces a code of conduct found at no other place of pilgrimage that I have ever visited.

It begins at the bronze statue of the Virgin welcoming visitors with

The arches where water from the spring is dispensed

outstretched arms. Dating from 1867, the statue had belonged to a religious community in Izmir, who presented it as a gift to Father François Saulais, the chaplain of Meryemana. Father Saulais had it installed on its plinth in 1960. Beyond the statue, down the long walkway escorted by the olive trees planted by Father Jung's men in the 1890s, lies the house itself. Up behind it and to the left is the raised bank where religious services are held by members of all faiths.

The entrance to the house, shaded by a large tree, leads into a small vestibule. On the side walls are two marble plaques – one in Turkish and one in French – honoring Sister Grancey, Fathers Jung and Poulin, and Archbishops Timoni and Descuffi. Passing through the archway into the main room, one enters a space of stark simplicity, with a high window on either side and usually a bank of flickering candles against each wall. The room is then divided by another archway, beneath which,

Above, a view of the exterior from the south
Left, the bronze statue of the Virgin that welcomes visitors to the site

embedded in the floor, is a large black marble tile marking the spot where the fireplace was found. Beyond that is the altar with a statue of the Virgin above it in the apse. This statue was found among the ruins of the house when it was first discovered, but it disappeared twice during the years when the house was a virtual prisoner of war; it was only rediscovered after the house had been handed back to the Lazarists in 1931. On each side of the altar is a niche, the one to the left containing the bronze lamp presented by Pope Paul VI during his visit in 1967.

Through the archway to the right is Mary's bedchamber, with only slivers of light coming through its high windows. On the back wall is a painting of the face of Mary executed directly on to the stone surface by the French painter Ratislas Loukine on a visit to the house in 1978. On the other walls are framed verses from the Koran relating to Mary.

Interior view

Because of the special status accorded to Mary in Islam, Muslims are often seen performing *namaz* (praying) in this room.

Back outside, the steps in front of the house lead down to the level where the *amasya* (holy water) comes out from taps in the arches that have been built into the mountainside. Unfortunately, the stonework around the arches is usually disfigured by a rash of chewing gum left stuck to the stones by people who have come to drink from the spring and felt the need to leave behind something, however unsightly, to commemorate their visit. Further along the wall is a series of metal grids to which Turkish Muslim pilgrims have attached little pieces of cloth representing the wishes they hope will be granted, the prayers they hope will be answered.

And are these prayers ever answered? Here one must tread carefully,

Ratislas Loukine's portrait of Mary painted in 1978 directly on to the stone wall of the house